# PARASITES

# Bedbugs

**Other titles in the Parasites series include:**

# PARASITES

# Bedbugs

## Shelley Bueche

**KIDHAVEN PRESS**

*An imprint of Thomson Gale, a part of The Thomson Corporation*

**THOMSON**

**GALE**

Detroit • New York • San Francisco • San Diego • New Haven, Conn. • Waterville, Maine • London • Munich

Picture Credits: Cover: Biophoto Associates/ Photo Researchers, Inc.; © Anthony Bannister; Gallo Images/CORBIS, 14; © Bettmann/CORBIS, 18; Biophoto Associates/Photo Researchers, Inc., 28; Dr. Tony Brain /Photo Researchers, Inc., 22; Corel, 27; Eye of Science/Photo Researchers, Inc., 13; Courtesy of Richard "Bugman" Fagerlund, 10; © Dr. Ken Greer/Visuals Unlimited, 15 (below); Courtesy of Harold Harlan, 19 (inset); Courtesy of Dr. Richard Houseman, 19 (below); © Dr. Dennis Kunkel/Visuals Unlimited, 9; © Dr. David M. Phillips/Visuals Unlimited, 8; Photos.com, 12; Sinclair Stammers/Photo Researchers, Inc., 20; Volker Steger/Photo Researchers, Inc., 7; Andrew Syred/Photo Researchers, Inc., 25

**LIBRARY OF CONGRESS CATALOGING-IN-PUBLICATION DATA**

Bueche, Shelley.

  Bedbugs / by Shelley Bueche.

    p. cm. — (Parasites)

  Includes bibliographical references and index.

  ISBN 0-7377-3168-0 (hard cover : alk. paper)

  1. Bedbugs—Juvenile literature. I. Title. II. Series.

  QL523.C6B84 2005

  595.7'54—dc22

                                          2004026042

# CONTENTS

# CHAPTER 1

# Bedbugs Are Parasites

**B**edbugs and millions of other bugs, beetles, flies, and cockroaches are members of the insect world. The common bedbug is a **parasite**. The word *parasite* comes from the Greek *para*, meaning "beside," and *sitos*, meaning "food." The word translates as "one who eats at another's table." This is an apt name, since a parasite can survive only by living off a **host**.

Bedbugs belong to the family of bloodsucking bugs. Bedbugs prefer human blood, but if they cannot find a person to attack, they will also feed on birds, rabbits, or bats.

Bedbugs do not have wings. They do not fly, but crawl everywhere on their six legs. Flat and oval shaped, these small bugs are only one-quarter of an inch (0.5 cm) long, about the size of an apple seed. Bedbugs have poor eyesight. To help them see and smell where they are going, they use their sensitive **antennae**. The antennae detect warmth and smell, allowing the bedbug to follow these senses to guide it.

*This magnified image of a bedbug shows the parasite's eyes, its six legs, and its two antennae.*

# Body of a Bedbug

**Bedbugs use their sharp, beaklike mouthparts to pierce a host's skin and feed on the host's blood.**

**Bedbugs have three pairs of legs for crawling and searching for food.**

**Bedbugs have flat, oval-shaped bodies.**

**Sensitive antennae help bedbugs see and smell.**

**Bedbugs are only one-quarter of an inch long.**

# Life Cycle

A female bedbug can lay five eggs a day and may lay up to 500 eggs during her lifetime. The female bedbug lays her eggs in a sticky substance that helps the eggs stay in place. The eggs hatch in one to two weeks. When hatched, the bedbug is no bigger than a pinhead. Young bedbugs, which are called nymphs, go through five stages of development. A bedbug must eat a meal before each life stage. Once a bedbug is ready for the next stage, it **molts**, or loses its skin. The development stages take place across six to eight weeks. After five molts, the nymphs reach **maturity**.

Young bedbugs look like adults, but they are lighter in color and smaller in size. All bedbugs are small and flat.

Adult bedbugs live from three to twelve months. They can live for several months without eating. In a single year three or four generations of bedbugs from

*The bedbug's blood-sucking mouthparts can clearly be seen in this magnified image.*

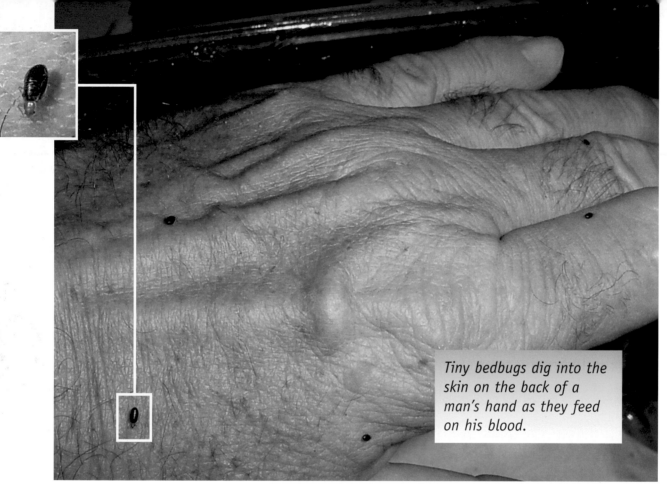

Tiny bedbugs dig into the skin on the back of a man's hand as they feed on his blood.

one family will be born and grow into adults. Bedbugs can lay eggs only in warm conditions. The warmer a place is, the faster bedbugs can multiply. A single female can lay enough eggs to infest a home.

# CHAPTER 2

# Good Night, Sleep Tight, Don't Let the Bedbugs Bite!

**B**edbugs get their name because they like to eat, sleep, and hide in warm, cozy places, such as beds. These bugs are known as "hitchhikers" because they can travel from a suitcase to a hallway and finally to a bed. These bugs hitch rides around the world on airplanes, trains, automobiles, and even cruise ships.

Bedbugs are good at hiding. They might hide behind a picture frame, inside an alarm clock, or behind a chair during the daytime. But when the sun goes down, bedbugs crawl to the nearest warm body and dig right in.

## Nocturnal Creatures

The early morning hours, between 3:00 A.M. and 4:00 A.M., are when bedbugs are out and about. Because they are **nocturnal**, bedbugs are usually not noticed.

*Bedbugs get their name because they like to live in warm, cozy places such as beds.*

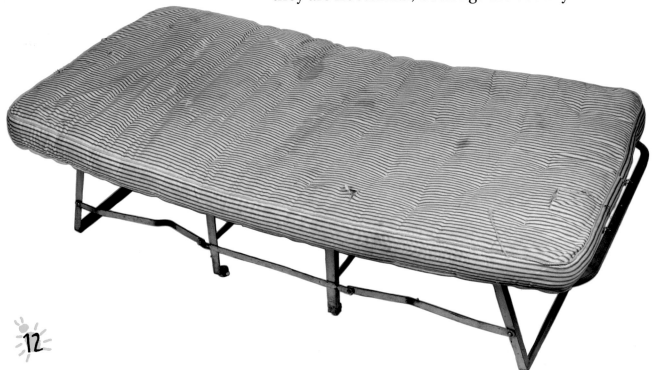

Bedbugs typically feed at night. Here, two bedbugs crawl along a mattress in search of a host to feed on.

## Mealtime

Nighttime is mealtime for bedbugs. Bedbugs look for a moist patch of skin on a host for their meal. They **insert** their sharp beak into the skin and drink blood from the host. When a bedbug is feasting on blood it injects **saliva** that produces irritation in the host. That saliva keeps blood from clotting so the bug can eat for longer periods of time.

A young nymph can drink blood for only three minutes before it is full. An adult bedbug can drink

*The body of a bedbug swells with blood as the parasite feeds on a host.*

blood for up to fifteen minutes. Once it has eaten, its body swells up to six times its original size. The bedbug looks like it is going to pop, just like a balloon. It turns a dark red. After eating, bedbugs carefully crawl off to hide out, **digest** their meals, and fall asleep for a long nap. Generally bedbugs do not travel far from their host.

Most people do not notice anything when a bedbug is feasting on them. The bite is painless, and a person might not even wake up while he or she is being bitten.

# Painful Welts

It is not until the next day that the host sees a hard, round, itchy **welt** on his or her skin. This itching can last from several hours to a few days. Sometimes these welts become infected and need to be treated with **antibiotic** cream.

A bedbug's bite leaves behind red, itchy welts like these on the skin of its host.

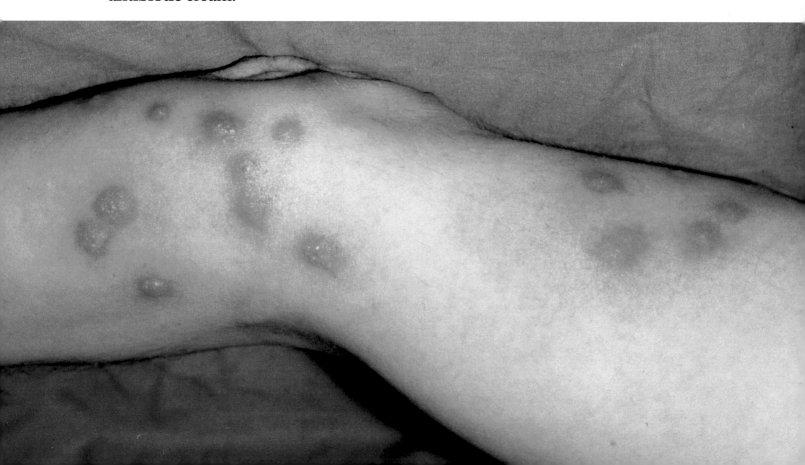

One way to recognize a bedbug **infestation** is by the sweet, minty smell released by their sweat glands, which is frequently left behind by the bugs. If an area is infested by these pests, often brown spots, or **excrement,** are left behind on sheets or clothing. The sneaky nighttime attacks make bedbugs a difficult enemy to defeat.

# CHAPTER 3

# Bedbugs Around the World

**B**edbugs have been pests to mankind since the beginning of time. In fact, scientists believe they were probably around when early people lived in caves.

Bedbugs were a very common problem for people until World War II. After the war, strong **pesticides** such as DDT were used worldwide and bedbugs were almost eliminated. Now, bedbugs are making

a comeback all over the world. This is partly because instead of pesticides, farmers are using bait to trap and kill unwanted insects. Bedbugs feed on blood and are not attracted to most types of bait used to trap other insects.

# Bedbug Invasions Everywhere

## From Five-Star Hotels

Bedbugs prey on the rich and the poor alike. They are found in a rundown motel as easily as in the finest five-star hotel in the world. In fact, Requejo Ventura, a businessman from Mexico, sued the Helmsley Park

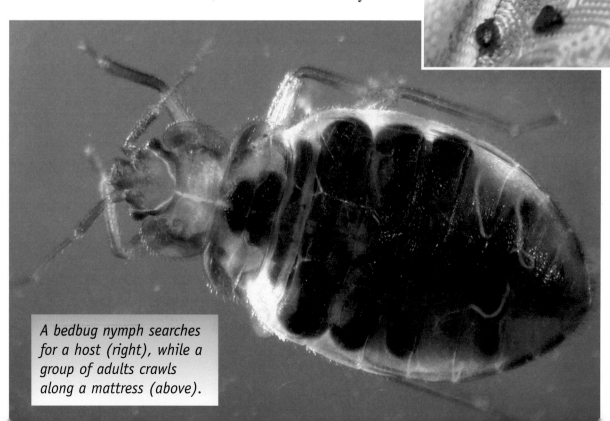

A bedbug nymph searches for a host (right), while a group of adults crawls along a mattress (above).

Bedbugs infest hotels, university dormitories, and homes across the world, where they thrive on human hosts.

Lane Hotel, a fancy hotel in New York City, after a sleepless night caused by a bedbug attack. The hotel moved Ventura to another room, but it was too late. The bugs had moved into Ventura's suitcase and traveled all the way back to Mexico with him, infesting his house.

## To University Dormitories in the United States

Another unusual bedbug story happened to college students at Tulane University in New Orleans, Louisiana. One at a time, microscopic bedbugs began falling out of the bricks at Butler House dormitory. Students thought they were living in a real-life horor movie. The bedbug problem got so bad that two of the college's dormitories had to be shut down during the summer of 2002.

## To a Schoolteacher's Home in Jacksonville, Florida

A more common bedbug story can be told by Shannon and her four children. The family started waking up with red welts on their arms and legs. The only thing that relieved the constant itching was to take a shower. After many trips to their family doctor, they finally realized they had a major bedbug problem in their home. After seven weeks of investigating, hunting for problems areas, and **fumigating** for the bugs, they were finally ready to move back home. The pests are gone, but the family still has nightmares about their experience with these tiny bedbugs!

*This close-up of a bedbug's profile shows one of its antennae and the long, sharp tube it uses to suck blood.*

## To the Outback in Australia

**Entomologists** in Sydney, Australia, have reported an 800 percent increase in bedbug invasions since the year 2000. It used to be that Australian scientists were the only ones noticing bedbug appearances, but now it seems that everyone is paying attention! Christmas is the time most bedbugs are spotted in Australia, because of the increase in tourists visiting for the holidays.

Not only are bedbugs making a comeback worldwide, but it appears that they are here to stay. Fortunately, there are ways to prevent bedbugs from making an appearance in your home.

# Getting Rid of Those Nighttime Critters!

**F**or a bug no bigger than a pencil eraser, these pests sure can cause a lot of agony. Now that bedbug infestations are on the rise around the world, it is a good idea for travelers to carefully **inspect** their luggage before leaving on a trip. Also, travelers should check their hotel rooms carefully before turning off the lights at night. They should look under the bed mattress, pillows, and even furniture for any telltale signs of bedbugs.

## Controlling Bedbug Invasions

In your own home, it is easier to prevent bedbug invasions or at least stop bedbugs from spreading. First, if you have a bedbug problem, wash all bedspreads, sheets, and curtains in very hot water. Dry them in the dryer at the highest temperature possible. Next, dust off all items in the room and make sure that every spot has been cleaned. Vacuum your carpet, going over every inch of the floor several times to pick up any bedbug eggs that may have been left behind. It is a good idea to vacuum your bed mattress, too, since this is where those bugs often hide out.

Once you have cleaned all the bug-infested rooms, get out a flashlight. A flashlight will help you check dark corners and cracks that you may have missed while cleaning. If you do find a small corner with just a few of these pests, tell your parents. They can spray the area with bug spray. Use the spray only in places where you find bedbugs hiding out. Never use bug spray on your clothes or near your bed. It is important to read all the directions first, and if you do not understand something, call a professional bug service for advice.

# Check the Attic!

Bats and birds can carry bedbugs with them when they nest in an attic. Once bedbugs are in this warm environment, they begin to multiply and spread to other rooms quickly. These bedbugs scamper into the other rooms of the house through walls and vents.

# Check the Temperature

Bedbugs are very sensitive creatures sometimes simply turning the temperature too high or too low may make bedbugs dash to a more comfortable environment. Temperatures above 100°F (38°C) or below 40°F (4.5°C) make these bugs uncomfortable.

# Eliminate Clutter

Another way to help cut down on the chances of bringing unwanted bedbug populations into your home is to keep all areas clean and free of clutter. If you bring secondhand items into your home, check that they are free of insects before you bring them inside.

# Call In the Experts!

Most professionals agree that totally **eliminating** bedbugs is not easy. Because these pests are so good at hiding and adapting to any environment, bedbugs are becoming a problem for more people than ever before.

Entomologist Harold Harlan recommends taking quick action with bedbug problems: "Some travelers wipe a small alcohol swab along the edges of their luggage after they have closed each piece, and then let that dry." Harlan says that "if there are bugs or their eggs on those edges, the alcohol is very likely to kill or dislodge them and removing them is very important in getting rid of them and preventing biting."

## The Mysterious Bedbugs

Although bedbugs are not known to spread disease, they are a major pest and can cause anxiety and **insomnia**. For most of us, though, bedbugs are simply an annoyance.

*In addition to bats, birds nesting in an attic can introduce bedbugs into the home.*

*Keeping your home clean and free of clutter is one of the best ways to prevent bedbug infestations.*

It is because these pests hide out during the day, only to attack us when we are fast asleep, that we dread these pests. The more we learn about bedbugs in our environment, the more we will know how to avoid them.

# GLOSSARY

**antibiotic:** A chemical that kills bacteria.

**antennae:** Feelers on the head of insects that help them to find their way around.

**digest:** To break down food into smaller parts, so it can be used by the body.

**eliminating:** Getting rid of something.

**entomologists:** Scientists who study bugs.

**excrement:** Waste discharged from the body.

**fumigating:** Spraying chemicals to get rid of pests.

**host:** A person or animal on which a parasite lives.

**infestation:** A large group of bedbugs or other insects living in one area, such as a person's home.

**insert:** To put into something.

**insomnia:** A condition that makes a person unable to get to sleep.

**inspect:** To carefully examine something or someone.

**maturity:** The adult stage in a bedbug's life.

**molt:** To shed old skin and grow new skin.

**nocturnal:** Only active at nighttime.

**parasite:** An insect that uses a person or an animal for food and sometimes shelter.

**pesticides:** Chemicals used to kill unwanted pests.

**saliva:** A liquid produced in the mouth.

**welt:** A swelling on the skin caused by a bedbug bite.

## Books

Christopher Maynard, *Micro Monsters: Life Under the Microscope.* New York: DK, 1999. This book for young researchers is from the Eyewitness Readers series. It provides a fascinating look at tiny creatures, including the bedbug, with color microscopic photographs.

Sara Swan Miller, *True Bugs: When Is a Bug Really a Bug?* New York: Franklin Watts, 1998. This introduction to true bugs includes detailed descriptions of fourteen species of insects, along with bedbugs, plus how to find, identify, and observe these true bugs.

## Web Sites

**AES Bug Club for Young Entomologists** (www.ex.ac.uk/bugclub). This Web site includes a page to ask a bug question, a bug club, and a newsletter. A great place to conduct further research on bedbugs and other insects.

**National Geographic Kids** (www.national geographic.com/ngkids). For general information about the insect world, there is no greater online resource than nationalgeographic.com. This interactive site includes games, puzzles, movies, animal photos, and downloadable files to search.

**National Pest Management Association (NPMA)** (www.pestworld.org). A one-stop online resource for information, facts, and research material on pests. Articles and facts on bedbugs, also known as Cimex lectularius. Be sure to check out: www.pestworldforkids.org for facts on pests from A–Z, just for kids.

# ABOUT THE AUTHOR

Shelley Bueche is a freelance writer, the author of numerous articles and one book, *The Ebola Virus,* published by KidHaven Press in 2003. She enjoys researching interesting bug facts, and one of her all-time favorite activities is chasing lightning bugs, with her two sons and three dogs, on hot summer evenings. She has a background in library science and materials for young adults. To learn more about the author, visit her Web site at: www.shelleybueche.smartwriters.com.